Pre-Decodable Takehome Books

Level Pre-K
Pre-Decodable Books 1-20

A Division of The McGraw-Hill Companies

Columbus, Ohio

www.sra4kids.com

SRA/McGraw-Hill

A Division of The McGraw·Hill Companies

2005 Imprint

Printed in the United States of America.

Send all inquiries to:
SRA/McGraw-Hill
4400 Easton Commons
Columbus, OH 43219

ISBN 0-07-584239-4
12 WCE 10

Contents

About the Pre-Decodable Takehome Books

The *SRA Open Court Reading Pre-Decodable Takehome Books* allow your children to apply their knowledge of phonic elements to read simple, engaging texts. Each story supports instruction in a new phonic element and incorporates elements and words that have been learned earlier.

The children can fold and staple the pages of each *Pre-Decodable Takehome Book* to make books of their own to keep and read. We suggest that you keep extra sets of the stories in your classroom for the children to reread.

How to make a Pre-Decodable Takehome Book

1. Tear out the pages you need.

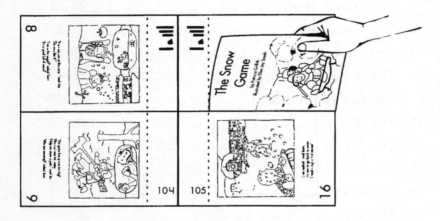

2. Place pages 4 and 5, and pages 2 and 7 faceup.

3. Place pages 4 and 5 on top of pages 2 and 7.

4. Fold along the center line.

Dragons Don't Get Colds

5. Check to make sure the pages are in order.

6. Staple the pages along the fold.

Stapler

Dragons Don't Get Colds

Just to let you know...

A message from _____

Help your child discover the joy of independent reading with *SRA Open Court Reading*. From time to time your child will bring home his or her very own *Pre-Decodable Takehome Books* to share with you. With your help, these stories can give your child important reading practice and a joyful shared reading experience.

You may want to set aside a few minutes every evening to read these stories together. Here are some suggestions you may find helpful:

- Do not expect your child to read each story perfectly, but concentrate on sharing the book together.
- Participate by doing some of the reading.
- Talk about the stories as you read, give lots of encouragement, and watch as your child becomes more fluent throughout the year!

Learning to read takes lots of practice. Sharing these stories is one way that your child can gain that valuable practice. Encourage your child to keep the *Pre-Decodable Takehome Books* in a special place. This collection will make a library of books that your child can read and reread. Take the time to listen to your child read from his or her library. Just a few moments of shared reading each day can give your child the confidence needed to excel in reading.

Children who read every day come to think of reading as a pleasant, natural part of life. One way to inspire your child to read is to show that reading is an important part of your life by letting him or her see you reading books, magazines, newspapers, or any other materials. Another good way to show that you value reading is to share a *Pre-Decodable Takehome Book* with your child each day.

Successful reading experiences allow children to be proud of their new-found reading ability. Support your child with interest and enthusiasm about reading. You won't regret it!

my  airplane

8

SRA
OPEN COURT READING

My Toys

by Grant Davis
Illustrated by Deborah Colvin Borgo

SRA

A Division of The McGraw-Hill Companies

Columbus, Ohio

my

ball

my
bike

my
doll

my

truck

my

teddy bear

the
family

The Family

by Seamus Waibel
Illustrated by Gary Undercuffler

A Division of The McGraw-Hill Companies

Columbus, Ohio

www.sra4kids.com

SRA/McGraw-Hill

*A Division of The **McGraw·Hill** Companies*

Send all inquiries to:
SRA/McGraw-Hill
8787 Orion Place
Columbus, OH 43240-4027

the
baby

the
father

the
boy

the
girl

4

the
mother

the

family

8

The Picnic

by Radley Womack

Illustrated by Meryl Henderson

SRA

A Division of The McGraw·Hill Companies

Columbus, Ohio

and my

uncles

my

aunts

6

the

picnic

3

 my
grandmothers

and my
grandfathers

my  friends

SRA OPEN COURT READING

Friends

by Tabitha Huxley
Illustrated by Loretta Lustig

A Division of The McGraw·Hill Companies

Columbus, Ohio

and a

cat

a
girl

the
girl

a
girl

and a
grandmother

my  pets

My Pets

by Max Caesar
Illustrated by Loretta Lustig

SRA

A Division of The McGraw·Hill Companies

Columbus, Ohio

in the

box

my
cat

my
pets

my
dog

in the
washtub

the **police officer**

The Police Officer

by Arlie MacPherson
Illustrated by Meryl Henderson

A Division of The McGraw-Hill Companies

Columbus, Ohio

my on the

brother   bike

the

police officer

4

the on the

police officer   bike

5

the fire truck

8

The Fire Truck

by Marlene Caplan
Illustrated by Meryl Henderson

A Division of The McGraw-Hill Companies

Columbus, Ohio

A  is in the .

girl   fire truck

the

fire truck

My is in the .

dog   fire truck

the

letters

The Letters

by Gertrude Paluch
Illustrated by Barry Mullins

A Division of The McGraw·Hill Companies

Columbus, Ohio

The [letters] are in my [hand].

the
letters

6

3

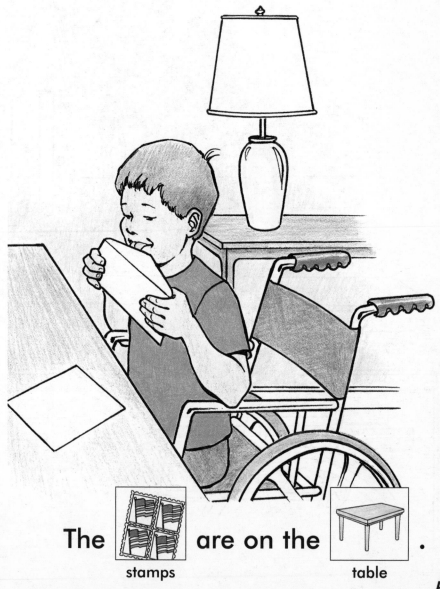

The are on the .

stamps

table

the

airplane

8

The Airplane

by Arleen James
Illustrated by Loretta Lustig

A Division of The McGraw·Hill Companies

Columbus, Ohio

You are on the  **.**

airplane

the airplane

You are in the ⬜ .

airport

the and the

car   boat

The Car and the Boat

by Gretchen Weller
Illustrated by Len Ebert

SRA

A Division of The McGraw·Hill Companies

Columbus, Ohio

You have a in the .

boat

water

7

the and the [boat]

car   boat

You have a in the .

car   garage

4

5

SRA OPEN COURT READING

the

bikes

8

The Bike

by Kristen John
Illustrated by Len Ebert

A Division of The McGraw-Hill Companies

Columbus, Ohio

SRA Open Court Reading

www.sra4kids.com

SRA/McGraw-Hill

A Division of The ***McGraw-Hill*** *Companies*

Printed in the United States of America.

Send all inquiries to:
SRA/McGraw-Hill
8787 Orion Place
Columbus, OH 43240-4027

You and I have  bikes

in my  garage .

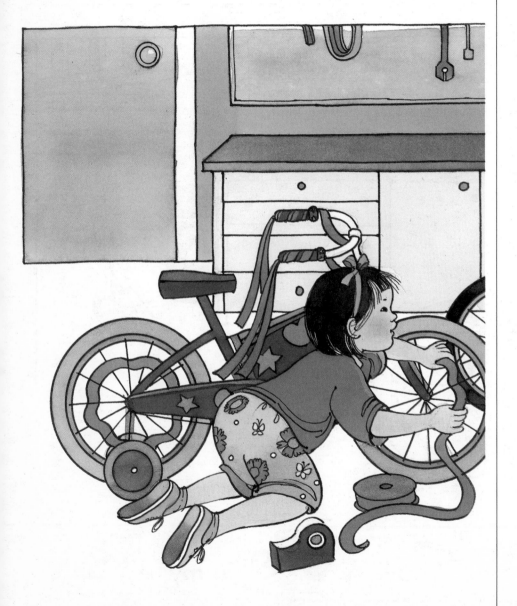

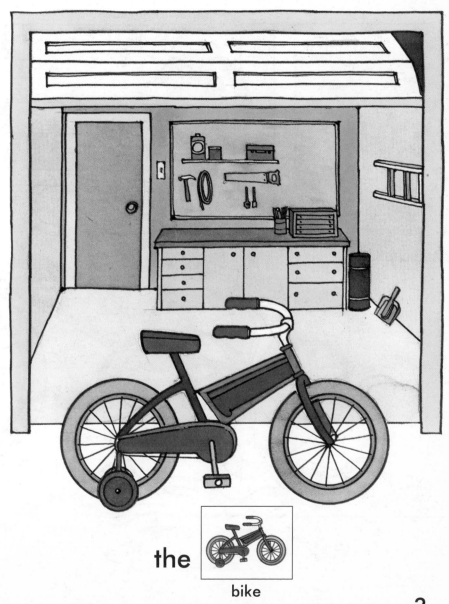

the

bike

I have a  in my  .

bike

garage

4

5

the

beach

SRA OPEN COURT READING

The Beach

by Dennis Linn
Illustrated by Len Ebert

A Division of The McGraw-Hill Companies

Columbus, Ohio

www.sra4kids.com

SRA/McGraw-Hill

A Division of The McGraw-Hill Companies

Copyright © 2003 by SRA/McGraw-Hill.

Printed in the United States of America.

Send all inquiries to:
SRA/McGraw-Hill
8787 Orion Place
Columbus, OH 43240-4027

He and I are in the .

water

the

boy

He is on the  .

beach

the
train

The Train

by Kevin Richards
Illustrated by Meryl Henderson

A Division of The McGraw-Hill Companies

Columbus, Ohio

She and I are on the .

train

the

girl

She is on the .

train

4

5

SRA OPEN COURT READING

the

cook

8

The Cook

by Sammy Miller
Illustrated by Olivia Cole

SRA
A Division of The McGraw·Hill Companies
Columbus, Ohio

He was ⬚ .

cooking

the

cook

6

3

The was in the .

cook   kitchen

4

5

the

farm

8

The Farm

by Rachel Bratter
Illustrated by Meryl Henderson

SRA

A Division of The McGraw·Hill Companies

Columbus, Ohio

The is at the .

horse   barn

the
farmer

6

3

The is at the .

farmer   farm

4

5

the and the

cows   ducks

The Cows

by Lyn Chang
Illustrated by Meryl Henderson

A Division of The McGraw-Hill Companies

Columbus, Ohio

The are with the .

cows

ducks

7

the

cows

6

3

The are with the .

cows

farmer

4

5

the

farm

8

The Lamb and the Chick

by Linda Huston
Illustrated by Olivia Cole

SRA

A Division of The McGraw·Hill Companies

Columbus, Ohio

www.sra4kids.com

SRA/McGraw-Hill

A Division of The McGraw·Hill Companies

Copyright © 2003 by SRA/McGraw-Hill.

Printed in the United States of America.

Send all inquiries to:
SRA/McGraw-Hill
8787 Orion Place
Columbus, OH 43240-4027

I had a [chick] in my [hand].

chick   hand

6

the

farm

3

I had a  in the .

lamb

barn

SRA OPEN COURT READING

the

mirror

8

The Mirror

by Sheryl Wolf
Illustrated by Meryl Henderson

A Division of The McGraw-Hill Companies

Columbus, Ohio

SRA OPEN COURT READING

I see my in the .

teeth   mirror

6

the  mirror

3

I see my in the .

nose   mirror

4

5

the

pie

The Pie

by Margaret Murray
Illustrated by Meryl Henderson

A Division of The McGraw-Hill Companies

Columbus, Ohio

The ⬜ is for my ⬜ .

pie   family

the  apples

The  are for the .

apples

pie

4

5

the
pond

8

The Pond

by Beverly Jeffrey
Illustrated by Len Ebert

A Division of The McGraw·Hill Companies

Columbus, Ohio

www.sra4kids.com

SRA/McGraw-Hill

A Division of The **McGraw·Hill** Companies

The is by the [ ] .

frog   pond

6

the  pond

3

He and I are by the  .

pond

4

5